The Undercliff Swimming Club's hut in Myrtle Bay, not long after it was constructed in the later 1880s. It had a small veranda along its frontage, with just a single door to gain access inside. The beach here was once quite sandy, but became progressively more boulder-strewn over time. In the twentieth century, the hut became commonly known as the Old Boathouse, or 'Britannia's Hut', after Olivia Parkes who lived in it for nearly thirty years, 'Britannia' being the name adopted by herself. (image courtesy Robert Trowbridge)

Front cover shows 'Britannia' (Olivia Parkes) just coming out on to the balcony of her home around 1950. The hut or boathouse was by then in a state of serious disrepair, virtually no maintenance having been done upon it for almost 40 years. (VHC – Brookes deposit)

BRITANNIA:
THE EXTRAORDINARY LIFE OF
OLIVIA PARKES
VENTNOR, ISLE OF WIGHT

MICHAEL FREEMAN
AND
ROBERT TROWBRIDGE

ISBN 978-0-9574514-1-4

• • • • •

Designed & Printed by: Meridian 3, Isle of Wight
www.meridian3.co.uk

Distributed by: W.J. Nigh & Sons, Shanklin, Isle of Wight PO37 7HX
www.wjnigh.co.uk

• • • • •

TABLE OF CONTENTS

· · · · ·

Looking westward along the Undercliff coastline towards Steephill in the distance, the beach here heavily boulder-strewn and Britannia's Hut plain to see in Myrtle Bay. Ventnor beach is several hundred metres behind the camera. The date of the photo is unknown, but it is certainly in the middle decades of the twentieth century. (image courtesy Stefan Wells)

FOREWORD

She called herself 'Britannia Olivia' after opening a confectioner and tobacconist shop in Ventnor, Isle of Wight in 1920. Towards the end of her life, a reporter in a national newspaper in 1958 described her as 'The Old Lady of the Sea'. She was the daughter of a Walsall ironfounder, growing up in what was ostensibly a middle-class household. And yet Olivia May Parkes spent almost 30 of her later years living in an old boathouse on stilts in a small secluded bay just west of Ventnor, at the full mercy of wind and rain. Her abode had no running water, no sanitation and no electricity. But much worse was that no maintenance was done to it after about 1920. In such an exposed setting, the large wooden hut soon became dilapidated, no longer water-tight, most of its windows rotten and their glass broken. There was a hole in the roof and the handrails were missing from the steps and from the balcony entrance. Day after day, in her sixties and into her seventies, she would climb down those steps to fetch water, to buy paraffin, and to buy food. She would then climb back, a bag in each hand, carefully steadying her ascent. To Ventnor's summer holidaymakers, she became a focus of intense curiosity: many of them found it hard to believe how someone could live in such conditions. Local inhabitants were much more habituated to her mode of life, accepting her as one of quite a number of eccentric figures who lived among them. Schoolboys would taunt her and throw stones at her home, but she was often given help by the longshoremen families, while others offered occasional sustenance. Her old boathouse became known as 'Britannia's Hut' and many had no idea of her real name. Even twenty or thirty years after her death in 1962, she remained a very live historical figure, especially as holidaymakers returned to old haunts from their childhood days. Now, into the third decade of the twenty-first century, sixty years from her passing, Olivia attracts interest as someone who lived 'off-grid', an individual who pursued a life that did not conform.

The imposing street frontage of Ryde Town Hall, Isle of Wight, where Olivia Parkes appeared before Magistrates in 1942. The Justices sat in the Council Chamber, adding to the formality of hearings. (Image courtesy Ryde Social Heritage Group)

OLIVIA PARKES: BRITANNIA WAIVES THE RULES

It is wartime Britain on the last day of June 1942. The scene is the court room in Ryde Town Hall where the County Bench on the Isle of Wight, Sir Godfrey Baring presiding, is handling a case of a woman's persistent obstinacy. Appearing before the Bench is Olivia May Parkes, 60 years of age, a spinster, residing at the Old Boathouse, Myrtle Bay, Ventnor. She styled herself 'Britannia Olivia', and 'Britannia' was the name by which most locals knew her. But this has no validity in the eyes of the court. She has been summoned for the fourth time for remaining in the boathouse on the shore below the Western Cliffs just beyond the town of Ventnor, contrary to the Defence (General) regulations of 1939. She had failed to answer to the first court summons on 24th February. She appeared for the second summons on 28th February and was bound over to be of good behaviour for 12 months. Despite this, she had obstinately remained living in the boathouse. P.C. Riggs, from the local police station, had interviewed Miss Parkes several times over and explained the Defence regulations, the Military having declared she would not be granted a permit to continue living there in wartime. Her response was that she did not intend to take any notice. The property was hers. 'Nobody was going to put her out' was the answer given to the constable. She added that if she were to be compensated with up to £1000, she would definitely clear out of the Island. A police inspector gave evidence at the second hearing, informing the Bench that the steps up to the clifftop had been removed so as to deter enemy landing, with the result that Miss Parkes was marooned in the boathouse at high tide and the only way out for her was to walk some way along the shore across boulders. It was thus urgent that she found other accommodation for her own safety. P.C. Riggs's final interview with Miss Parkes was on April 8th when he found her still residing in the boathouse. Yet again, she asserted that this was her property, she could not get a house or lodgings, and so was staying, adding that 'it is only catty women who are trying to get me out of here'. P.C. Riggs told her that once more he would be reporting her conduct.

At the third court hearing, on 28th April, Sir Godfrey Baring reminded Miss Parkes that she was not permitted to remain in the boathouse by law. Miss Parkes replied by asking the Bench 'not to trample down a woman without finding things out'. She observed that some of the soldiers did not wish her to leave. She proceeded to make rambling statements about the various difficulties she had experienced, including the way children had sometimes pounded her home with stones. The Chairman told Miss Parkes that the Bench had listened to her with much patience, but it was a serious matter to defy the law. She was fined £3. If the fine was not paid, she would be sent to prison for one month.

Miss Parkes was before the court for a fourth time on 30th June 1942 having failed to pay the fine and for continuing to live in the boathouse. She pleaded not guilty but was nevertheless committed to prison for one month. On 1st July 1942, a report of her case appeared in the Portsmouth Evening News, and according to the news reporter, the Bench had agreed to take into account the defendant's mental and physical condition. It is not known whether Miss Parkes did actually serve the one-month sentence.

IN THE *County* OF *Southampton*
PETTY SESSIONAL DIVISION OF *the Isle of Wight*   **Register of the Court of Summary Jurisdiction,** sitting at

nber	Name of Informant or Complainant	Name of Defendant	Age of Defendant, if known	Nature of Offence, or of Matter of Complaint	Date of Offence
1	2	3		4	5
428	Harry Rogers	Constance Campbell	26	Breach of Lighting Restrictions Order	10 June
429	Harry Rogers	Richard Robert Dove	48	Keeping dog without a licence	
430	Harry Rogers	Olivia Parkes	60	Breach of Defence (General) Regs	
431	Ralph F. Close	Edward Jas McDonnell	41	False Pretences	

the Town Hall, Ryde, the 30th day of June 19 1942

Sum. Juris. Rule 3.

Plea	Minute of Adjudication	Time allowed for Payment and Instalment
6	7	8
N.A.L.	Fined 10/- & in default 7 days.	
N.A.	Fined 7/6 & in default	
Not Guilty	Committed for one month	
	Remanded in custody until Saturday 4th at Newport.	

The upper image shows the left-hand page of the court record of Olivia Parkes's appearance before the County Bench, sitting in Ryde Town Hall on 30th June 1942. She is case number 430, with the adjudication of the case recorded in the lower image, the right-hand page, third line down.
(images courtesy Isle of Wight Record Office, deposit reference: CPS/REG/8)

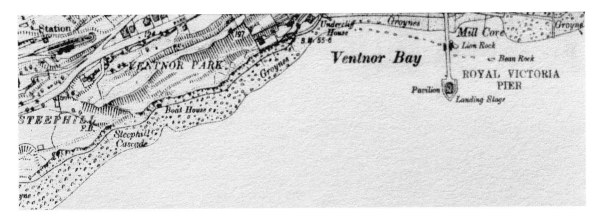

The location of the Old Boathouse is shown on this enlarged detail from a 1909 edition of an Ordnance Survey 6-inch map sheet. It was found just to the east of Steephill Cascade, roughly on the High Water Mark, and is about a quarter of a mile from Undercliff House which marks the western edge of Ventnor beach. There were steps down to the boathouse from the cliff walk above. The Cascade was where Olivia often obtained fresh water. (VHC)

The 1942 court cases by and large replicated the attitudes that Olivia had displayed to all manner of authority since her arrival in the town, some twenty-two years earlier, when she opened a confectioner and tobacconist shop at the bottom of Pier Street. She repeatedly flouted shop trading laws, repeatedly failed to pay fines levied, or else delayed paying them to the last minute. She seemed unworried about getting into arrears on rent payments or on other debts that she accumulated. In the summer of 1920, she was summoned for a breach of the Shops (closing) Order. In evidence, P.C. Cooke stated that at 10.20 p.m. one evening he had stopped three people who had visited the defendant's shop and bought packets of chocolates and paid 3 shillings for them. The constable then interviewed the defendant on the matter, informing her that she was committing an offence by selling after 8 p.m. Her response to him was that she did not care about the law: 'she was there to oblige the public'. Olivia failed to appear in response to the summons and the Bench was informed that the defendant had been fined twice for similar contraventions earlier that same year, in one instance a fine of 10 shillings, and in the second a fine of 40 shillings. For this third offence, she was fined 50 shillings. She had also been repeatedly cautioned by local police on the same count, but 'absolutely ignored them' in the words of one of the police sergeants who gave evidence in court.

One of Olivia's earlier offences that year had caught the eye of John Bull, the weekly magazine, founded in 1820, that championed traditional, conservative and increasingly populist views. An open letter was printed on the 6th March 1920 addressed to Britannia Olivia Parkes, confectioner, Ventnor. It began as follows:

> *'DEAR MADAM, I don't know whether you are "Mrs" or "Miss", but you are certainly a bit of a wag. A sturdy policeman, having nothing better to do, dropped on you for selling sweets to a man at 9.45 on a Sunday night. You sent a little note to the Bench, pointing out that you held a refreshment-house licence to serve up to 10 p.m. and asking if that included the sale of cigarettes and chocolates, "as policemen seem to be the only people acquainted with the law". Further, you expressed your considered opinion that "it was disgusting the way people in England were dogmatised about", and that "the sooner the Bench got a move on and discovered the man who introduced the Act of 1917 and obliterated it, the better it would be".*

The putative reference to a law of 1917 relates to the Defence of the Realm Act 1914 (D.O.R.A) and the steps that were subsequently taken to address food shortages from 1916. This fixed the closing hours of shops on different days in an attempt to ensure shopkeepers traded fairly. After the war ended, some of the D.O.R.A regulations remained, including shop closing times and hence the reason for Olivia's prosecutions. It is estimated that there were almost a million prosecutions for breaches of this legislation. John Bull's piece of comic satire saw 'Britannia Olivia' as some kind of retail warrior, as well as a 'bit of a wag'. The magistrates in the case fined her ten shillings, after she had received two warnings, with John Bull remarking that she clearly had her 'money's-worth in fun'.

By 1923, it seems that Olivia is still engaged in contraventions of closing hours at her shop. The Portsmouth Evening News carried a column on 21st August that year which recorded how a local Constable had been keeping a watch on the shop and twice had had occasion to caution her for selling cigarettes after hours. On the third time, his patience had run out and she was summoned and fined

£5. It is unlikely that she attended court. Five years later, the Mercury recorded that in September 1928, she still had an unpaid fine for keeping her shop open after hours, the paper noting that she had been convicted five times previously for similar offences. By this time, the Ventnor Council had started to become quite exercised by Miss Parkes's repeated breaches of shop regulations. It was upsetting other shopkeepers and generating complaints on a regular basis. Council members wanted a warrant issued for her arrest if fines still went unpaid.

One thing that may offer an explanation for Olivia's recalcitrant attitude to regulation of shop opening hours is that she and her sisters had, according to a family member alive today, run a sweet shop in Walsall for a time. This was probably in the early 1900s when there was relatively little in the way of regulation of opening hours. In other words, the regulatory conditions that applied in the 1920s must have rather grated with Olivia, especially if she was on the cusp of insolvency at times. It may also have been the case that her profit from takings during illegal hours more than offset the accumulated fines.

Huts on the Eastern Esplanade about 1930. (Image courtesy Digweed family archive)

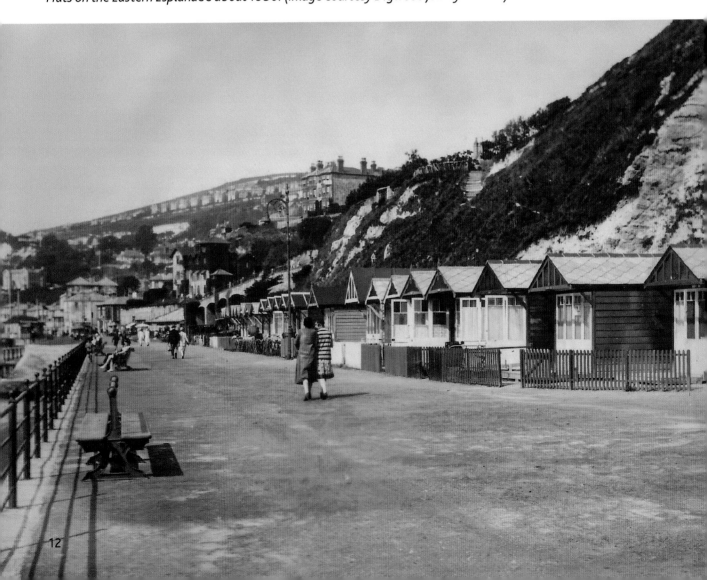

By 1929 or 1930, Olivia seems to have vacated the Pier Street shop and was living in beach hut number 30 on the Eastern Esplanade. That particular esplanade had been created in the late 1880s and, in the early decades of the twentieth century, the Council erected various huts at the base of the cliff slope, facing on to the Esplanade, that were available for visitors for day use. In 1921, a further set of huts, described as 'bungalows', were added, sometimes also listed as 'furnished', and with benefit of small fenced 'sitting-out areas'. Like the earlier huts, they were for day use only and could not be lived in or used as shops. It is clear that Olivia's hut number 30 was one of these.

It was only a matter of time before the Council registered that Olivia was actually residing in hut 30, but it was soon apparent that she was also using it as a shop and sometimes had a weighing machine outside. The local Council informed her in May 1930 that neither practice was permitted and she was told that, if she failed to comply with the terms of the tenancy agreement, her tenancy would be terminated immediately. She would later claim that she owned the hut. But this was untrue. There were times when the Council granted certain individuals block leases on some of the huts, including the 'bungalows', and those individuals then rented them out to holidaymakers. However, the Council remained the owner.

It seems that, for a while, Olivia complied, but when, in the early spring of 1932, a somewhat delinquent 11-year-old boy was charged by police on account of his wilfully damaging showcases and chests in that same hut, it becomes clear that she was still trading from it, if not living in it. In fact, the charge sheet for the boy stated that the owner of the damaged property was of Myrtle Bay, Ventnor, which means that, by that time, Olivia was living in the Old Boathouse there. This is also more or less confirmed by an incident reported in the Portsmouth Evening News in its issue of 11th November 1931. The paper described a 'Woman's Night of Terror' on a lonely beach west of Ventnor. 'Miss Olivia Parkes', living a 'life of seclusion' in an old boathouse on 'wooden pillars', had a terrifying night as heavy seas washed away the steps down from her 'weird place of abode'. She feared that the strength of the gale would wash the entire structure away. She spent almost a day marooned, but an errand boy heard her calling for help and, in due course, the fire brigade came to the rescue, using an auxiliary fire escape to bring her up the cliff and to a place of shelter. She must have returned to the boathouse to live there permanently sometime later in 1932, for the Council had forcibly removed her hut on the eastern Esplanade by then, in the light of persistent contraventions over its use. She was later to claim that it was removed by a traction engine and some of her things damaged in the process.

The image shows the south end of Pier Street in Ventnor, looking almost due north. Olivia's confectioner and tobacconist shop was on the extreme left, just out of camera view and beneath the wide canopy. The shop and the building are still there today, adjacent to the Baptist church. The residential accommodation above the shop was 32A. This particular image probably dates from about 1914. (VHC)

OLIVIA ACTING UP

There was something of the actress about Olivia Parkes, not just in terms of the way she saw herself, but equally significant, in the way she was viewed by others. In an advert for her Pier Street shop, posted in a concert programme of 1927, she described herself as 'Britannia Olivia', a 'high class' confectioner and tobacconist whose shop was open on Sundays (illegally, of course). She was using the 'Britannia' name at least as early as 1921, for it figures in the entry she made on the form for the British Census of that year (image courtesy National Archives). With the exception of the phrase 'own account', the writing reveals Olivia's own very distinctive hand, including artistic flourishes on most of the capitals.

The name is re-confirmed in Kelly's Directory for the Isle of Wight of 1924, the entry reading '32 Olivia Miss B. confectioner', 32 being the number of her premises on Pier Street. How far she thought of herself as the helmeted female warrior holding a trident and shield that came to form a personification of Britain, represented on the backs of coins and modelled in statue form across the kingdom, we will never know. But the choice of name does resonate with her numerous tussles with the law in which she displayed a tenacity and single-mindedness that equated with some kind of warrior spirit. Ultimately, the name 'Britannia' stuck for the rest of her life, many locals as well as visitors never knowing her by any other name. It became symbolic not just of character but of her chosen mode of living, a sentinel on Britannia's shore.

Ron Pusey was a young lad in Ventnor when Olivia opened her Pier Street shop around 1920. He was from a family that was always short of money and so he was for ever on the look-out for odd jobs. Soon he found himself doing regular errands for Olivia, remarking how she styled herself as 'Madame' or 'Madame Olivia'. She proved generous towards Ron, sometimes giving him 'old stock' chocolates that could be a bit fousty, but fine to eat if you wiped them off. She would occasionally also reward him with a 'threepenny bit' (a distinctive 12-sided coin that was bronze in colour and remained in circulation until 1964). This was no small sum at the time, enough to buy three bags of chips at a 'pennyworth' each. Mabel Allisstone also remembered Olivia from the 1920s. Her mother and father ran the Palmerston Hotel on Hambrough Road nearby and Mabel recalls that much of Olivia's shop was taken up by a grand piano. She was reputed to sleep under it, along with several cats. Mabel recalls being somewhat mesmerised by her, as were other youngsters: her iron grey and black curly hair seemed to terrify a few of the very young children. The shop that she rented was just a lock-up, without access to the rear living quarters or to the other accommodation upstairs (32A).

In the 1920s and well into the 1930s, Olivia would supplement her income by selling sweets and chocolates as well as apples and oranges on the cliffs and on the beach in summer, in the process gaining the nicknames 'Apple Annie' and 'Nell Gwyn', the latter after Charles II's famous mistress who, before she became legendary, sold oranges to fashionable audiences at London's new Playhouse theatre.

Even here, Olivia revealed no willingness to comply with the law, for selling on the beach and promenade was limited to whoever held the concession to do so (foreshore rights), with tenders invited every few years. In the early 1930s, the concession (upon an annual £8 payment) was exercised by Reg Flux whose family were established fruiterers in Ventnor. Typically, Reg would begin at one end of the beach, only later to discover that Olivia had begun selling at the other end. They would eventually meet in the middle and an argument would ensue.

Olivia was remembered by some holidaymakers during the 1930s as a somewhat rotund lady, dressed in shapeless dark clothing and hat, and always carrying a large wicker basket, rather similar to the ones used by the fishermen. Just as the chocolates she offered Ron Pusey were sometimes a bit 'past their sell by date' in modern terminology, so the fruit she plied could be a bit over-ripe, some of it the discarded stock of the town grocers. Few locals ever bought items from her basket for this reason. Some of the local kids confessed, when recalling Olivia much later in life, to having been slightly scared by her appearance. One former lad still alive today describes her hair as a bit like 'last year's bird's nest'. But there is sometimes no accounting for the perceptions of youngsters.

The children with the more vivid imaginations thought that Olivia might possibly be a witch, and her unusual, 'eyrie-like', seaside abode, fifteen feet up in the air on an isolated part of the sea-shore, added to the perception, even more so by the 1950s as the structure had signs of chronic decay, both from the action of the elements and from the damage to the hut's roof that followed years of older children pounding it with stones from above. The stone-throwing seems to have started just before the war and gained in frequency after Ventnor Secondary School was evacuated to nearby Steephill Castle in November 1940. Although the school kids were forbidden to venture down to the coast, and especially not in their lunch break, the ones living in and around Ventnor would often walk back home by the coast path which passed above Olivia's boathouse. Here they would practise hitting it with stones, largely boys not girls, with the bigger boys usually causing the most damage. If Olivia was home, she would come out on to the narrow landing and plead with them to stop or harangue them vigorously. After June 1942, of course, she was not permitted to live there any longer, which meant that the stone-throwing went wholly unchecked until she returned sometime during the last months of the war.

There were some youngsters, again when recalling Olivia late in their lives, who remarked how, on occasions, she would spend time talking to them, indicating that she had another rather different side to her. She came from a family where there were five other siblings, as we will discover, and most were younger. A result might well have been that Olivia could identify with the local kids who were intrigued and inquisitive about her unusual home. For them, the 'witch' was not what was in their minds at all. Instead, she lived in what, today, would be called a kind of tree house, a place where children pull up the ladder to hide away from the adults. It was an escape from being under the control of others, which meant as much to Olivia as it might have done to some of the kids.

There were, in fact, all sorts of stories that circulated over the years as to Olivia's life history. She was herself the source of some them, while others were loosely intelligent speculation as to why she spent nearly 30 years living in her seaside 'eyrie'. Rosemary Blake, wife of Jim Blake, one of Ventnor's leading longshoremen, recalled her claiming once that she was a Russian Princess. And by arriving in Ventnor in 1919, this was not altogether untenable, given that many of the Russian aristocracy had fled to Europe after the Bolshevik uprising the year before. Another story was that Olivia's husband had drowned in Myrtle Bay and so her 'eyrie' allowed her to keep a constant watch to his memory. Yet another was that Olivia forever mourned the loss of a sweetheart in the Great War and thus saw her seaside home, facing the sea across to France, as a way of salving that sorrow, always in the remote hope he might one day return. A young lad by the name of Philip Burton once saw Olivia standing on the beach near her wooden hut looking out. It was the summer of 1957 and he was on holiday with his family. Decades later, when the lad had become an adult and a successful poet, he wrote a piece under the title 'The Longest Wait'. It related the story of a woman 'forever embayed between two headlands – for the love of a Great War soldier expected back'. It was the same story of a lost sweetheart, but still having currency long after Olivia's death.

Ventnor beach crowded with holidaymakers one summer between the wars. In July and August, there would be near standing room only on warm days. (image courtesy Digweed family archive)

A view of the boathouse looking east around the mid-1950s.
(image courtesy Sharon Champion)

Certain of these stories were eventually nailed by a reporter for the Daily Mail when he managed to be one of the very few people who ever gained entry to the boathouse. One day in 1956, Gordon Bick took the courage to seek out Miss Parkes, describing how he felt like Jack, of fairy tale fame, climbing the Beanstalk as he started to ascend the precarious wooden steps that led to her extraordinary seaside home on its 15-foot wooden piles. Knocking on the double doors, he eventually heard a shuffling and, instead of seeing a giant, saw a tiny, white-haired old lady in tattered clothes. 'Who are you?', she snapped, so Bick recorded. 'What do you want? I am not used to visitors'. There must have been something about Bick that persuaded Olivia Parkes to talk to him. He must have explained that he was a news reporter, for she quickly sought to tell him that the many stories about her were all untrue: she had not been married and she had not been jilted. She claimed (not true) that she had had the place built because she liked fresh air and being by the sea. She said her life was 'lovely 35 years ago' when she first came to Ventnor. She then had a sweet shop and was quite prosperous. But then she went bankrupt and came to live in the old boathouse. Her only friends were now the seagulls. The local Council had offered to find another place for her to live, but she declined. It was so peaceful being there, she added.

Having achieved a conversation that lasted longer than many others had done, Bick withdrew on to the narrow wooden ledge outside the double doors and clambered unsteadily back down the unrailed steps, leaving, in his words, Miss Parkes to go back like a winkle into her shell. What he then went on to report was the astonishing shambles that he had found once inside: old newspapers piled eight feet high, numerous stacks of small boxes, hundreds of empty tin cans, and loads of empty matchboxes. Bick registered that most of the glass in the four sets of windows had gone or was broken. Part of the roof had also caved in. She had a couch for a bed and, to keep dry, she had erected a large canvas cover above it, possibly an old sail provided by a kind longshoreman.

On a rough calculation, made from gauging the width of the doors and windows as revealed in photographs, we can say that the boathouse was around twenty feet long and eight feet wide. She used oil for heating, lighting and cooking, so the place was, on anyone's guess, a potential tinder-box. One can barely imagine what it would have been like in a south-westerly autumn or winter gale, with most of the window openings to west and south devoid of their glass, a hole in the roof, and the sea at high tide blasting against the oak piles, salt spray flying through the air. It would have been yet more terrifying in an electrical storm, the lightning flashes illuminating the open sea as in many an old master romantic painting. Few observers disagreed with the description often applied to Miss Parkes that she was 'a real tough nut'. But she was also someone who plainly yearned, in some measure, for a life of seclusion.

In her later years, press articles about Olivia's mode of living did repeatedly describe her as a recluse, but one young woman resident on Pier Street in the late 1940s and early 1950s remembers her as neither 'strange or peculiar'. She was just 'an ordinary everyday woman', typically 'minding her own business' as she shopped daily at the Co-op butcher at 30 Pier Street (right next to the sweet shop that she once ran) and at Island Dairies, for milk, butter and cheese, a few doors further up. Another young resident of the time, this time a child, recalls Olivia coming into the 'bookie' or betting shop in Spring Hill, Ventnor, where her mum worked. Sat under the counter so that she was largely out of sight of the punters, she was still able to gain a vivid image of Olivia, including the spotless white petticoats under her skirt and how she kept her money in her knicker leg. Betting shops at this time were illegal, but the local police appear to have taken a blind eye to this one, allegedly because they themselves frequented it. Olivia, of course, would not have been bothered in the least, given her much earlier record of non-compliance as a shopkeeper.

The label of her being a recluse does not really equate, either, with the many years she spent plying sweets and fruit to the public on Ventnor beach and on the cliff walks nearby. However, one is bound to wonder how she came to be so antagonistic towards any kind of authority. This was not inconsistent with being a recluse, but her vigorous refusal to follow any kind of rules, and her constant bridling against anyone or any institution that sought to tell her what she could and could not do is different. In her court statements when appearing before Sir Godfrey Baring in 1942 for failing to vacate the old boathouse in wartime, it was striking to hear her admit that she had been offered a room rent-free in the town, provided she helped with the work of the house. But she had declined that offer: 'she was not going to work for anyone'.

There are some clues to these facets of Olivia's behaviour in incidents and experiences from her much younger life. She seemed always fearful of finding things outside of her own control

This image demonstrates very powerfully the precarious position of Olivia's abode at high tide. The date the photo was taken is 1958, but judging from the appalling state of the rear roof slope, it is very possibly after she was forcibly re-housed in late October 1958.
(image courtesy Reginald Cox)

Walsall High Street circa 1900. The town was positioned on an eminence above the River Tame, 8 miles north of Birmingham and 6 miles east of Wolverhampton. It grew rapidly as an industrial centre in the mid-Victorian period, with a population over 70,000 by 1891. The Italian Renaissance Town Hall (1867) marked the first of a series of fine public buildings. The town had much open space, including an arboretum of 90 acres. Saddlery, tanning, currying and iron smelting were among its principal manufacturing activities. (image courtesy Walsall Archives)

EARLY LIFE IN WALSALL, STAFFORDSHIRE

Olivia May Parkes was born on 17th November 1881 at 11, Albert Street in Walsall, Staffordshire. Her mother, Olivia Eliza (née Gee) registered the birth on 28th December 1881. She was the second-born child, a four-year-old brother, Frank James, being the first from the marriage between Olivia Eliza and one Joseph Parkes. In due course, there were six children to the family: four girls and two boys.

Albert Street was close to the town centre, the main railway line running to its west. The property does not exist any longer and the area is now largely in mixed open use, cleared of buildings. At some point in Olivia's young life, the family moved to 150 Wednesbury Road, in what became an unambiguously middle-class area where fields on the town's outskirts had been newly released for house building. The 1891 Census gives Joseph Parkes as a malleable ironfounder, while his near neighbours included a wholesale clothier's buyer as one family head, a land agent/surveyor as another, and a further neighbour was a grocer.

The modern image (from Google Earth) shows some of the properties that formed part of this new terrace, with number 150 out of view to the right. As can be seen, the dwellings consisted of three storeys, probably with a cellar as well. There were as many as 6 bedrooms and the properties had rear access through the archways that interspersed every other individual dwelling. Such a house would have been a very comfortable place in which to raise a family of 6 children, 5 of whom are recorded in the 1891 census. They were Frank James aged 14, Olivia May, aged 9, William Summerfield aged 7, Kathleen Matilda, aged 4 and Nora Marguerette Josephine aged 1. The sixth-born child, Florence Mabel, came very soon after. Within the family, Olivia was always known as 'Cissy' and signed herself as such, William was known as 'Will', while Florence was called 'Flossie'.

We know little about Olivia's schooling or that of her siblings. There was a National School in nearby Hillary Street, but this was not opened till 1893. Another National School had opened on Palfrey Street in 1884 and would have been the more likely one for Olivia to attend. But she may have been sent to a private school, which were common at the time, and often favoured by families that were in trade. Olivia was remembered in her later years as well educated, well-spoken and well written, which would be consistent with attending a private school. Her very stylish handwriting also suggests a private education.

Photos of Olivia Eliza Gee and Joseph Parkes, taken in Walsall, probably around 1875, before their marriage the year following (images courtesy Doug Brock).

Olivia Eliza Parkes, with her eldest son, Frank James, daughter Olivia May, and youngest son William Summerfield, in a photo taken about 1885. Frank's sailor suit was then very fashionable apparel for young boys, with many such garments beginning to be mass-produced for sale in the new department stores of the period (image courtesy Lauren Johnstone)

Joseph Parkes, Olivia's father, in a studio photo taken around 1891 when he had become the new owner of the Blue Lane Foundry in Walsall, specialising in the manufacture of malleable iron castings. He had set up business on his own, after some twenty years learning the trade at his father's works (image courtesy Lauren Johnstone)

Olivia's father, Joseph, was the only son of William Salter Parkes, a Walsall ironfounder who operated from a site close to the main railway line, north-east of the centre of the town. It was known as the Excelsior Works in the Wisemore district, located on Albert Street. William Parkes and his family lived at Lime House on Littleton Street. In the 1871 Census, son Joseph was 18 years old and listed as a smith's assistant. Also in the household were William's wife Mary and 4 daughters, aged from 24 to 15. William Salter Parkes was aged 48 at the time, his wife was 49. The Excelsior Works is given in a local directory entry of 1870 as manufacturing 'pit cages, props, tub work, capplings, boring joints etc etc.' It also built railway carriages and undertook engine and machine smith work. Surviving plans of the works, dated 1882-1883, reveal them to comprise a corrugated iron structure, open on one side, with a large chimney stack and a yard. By the 1881 Census, Joseph Parkes is described now as an ironfounder, aged 28, still living on Albert Street. He was by then in partnership with his father and effectively managing the Excelsior Works. The signs are that it was a profitable enterprise, hence the move of Joseph and his growing family to the house in Wednesbury Road.

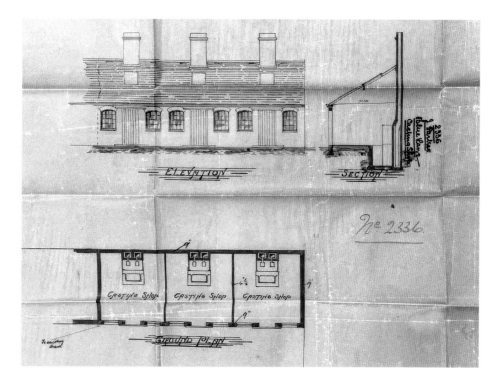

By about 1890, Joseph had moved to set up on his own, acquiring a more commodious casting works in Blue Lane East, adjacent to St. Patrick's Roman Catholic Church and Presbytery. The partnership with his father based at the Excelsior Works was dissolved in March 1890. The likelihood appears to be that his father, now in his late sixties, was partially retiring from business, although the public notice of the dissolution stated that he would be carrying on work as a 'smith'. Joseph agreed to buy out his father's share of the casting business and any other material assets for £1,200. This was arranged as a loan from his father on which Joseph would pay annual dividends from the profits of the Blue Lane Works. In 1891, Joseph had plans passed to extend the Blue Lane casting shops, apparently doubling them in size. The above surviving drawing of the extension indicates the scale and nature of the scheme. (image courtesy Walsall Archives).

For a while, it would appear that Joseph Parkes's new business met with some success, for in 1897 he was advertising in the Walsall Red Book, a prime trades directory of the period, as manufacturing 'The Very Best Malleable Iron Castings' (image courtesy Walsall Archives). Unfortunately, by 1901, Joseph Parkes's business had been declared bankrupt. It transpired that the annual dividend payments to his father had been made in only the first two years, and when his father, William Salter Parkes, died in 1897, the trustees of the estate pressed for payment of all outstanding dividends, despite having a power of postponement. One further payment was made, but subsequently, Joseph's business was unable to meet the full obligations. Joseph claimed that he had paid too high a price when buying out his father's partnership share. It seems, too, that he had suffered some bad debts, one of which was on a government contract to supply saddles, bridles and other ancillary items for the British Army in the Boer War. Orders had been placed, but without funds being provided in support. And when the war came to a swift end, the goods were no longer required. There was also an allegation at the bankruptcy adjudication that he had not kept regular financial records or employed someone else competent to do so. He stated that the new business had barely been solvent, although it is hard to establish whether or not this was really the case if accounts were not maintained correctly. Very strangely, it was claimed at the bankruptcy hearing that Joseph had no previous knowledge of the business, which was rather extraordinary given the length of time that he had worked in the trade alongside his father. Many years after, his daughter Kathleen was to record that her father was once a highly successful saddlery merchant and it was when the government failed to pay for their contract orders that all was lost.

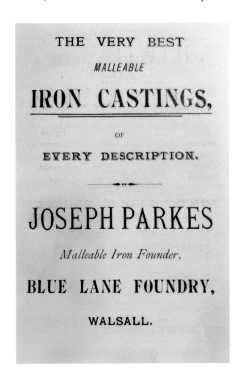

What may have compounded Joseph Parkes's difficulties was the death from pneumonia of his wife Olivia Eliza in June 1892, aged 40. He was left with six children, including several very young ones. The effect on 10-year-old Olivia May, the eldest daughter, must have been devastating. As a middle-class household, it is very likely that there had been help from a housemaid or a nursemaid and this probably continued for some years after the mother's death. Joseph's own mother may also have helped, as she lived nearby. But this was never going to replace the practical and emotional loss to the father and all the six children.

The creditors in the bankruptcy action eventually received 6s. 8d in the pound, but this would have been more than 10 shillings in the pound had the trustees of his father's estate not insisted on payment of the outstanding dividends. Joseph in fact claimed that his father, whilst alive, had not pressed for payment of the dividends. Moreover, William Salter Parkes, after he died in 1897, left estate valued at £883, a remarkable sum at the time, worth some £140,000 in today's money. The primary legatees were his wife and three daughters, Joseph himself being left a trifling share. One is left to wonder if father and son had fallen out.

What is also interesting is that the Blue Lane Foundry, under the name of Parkes & Co., continued to trade successfully under new ownership. In 1916, the proprietor was W.H. Tompkins, with telegrams to 'Parkes 189 Walsall'. It was producing much the same range of castings as it had under Joseph, indicating that here was a business with a well-established goodwill. His expansion of the business in 1891 was plainly not a rash decision. Eldest son, Frank, worked with him through the 1890s, and the stylish business card shown below has the hallmarks of a successful enterprise (image courtesy Doug Brock).

The eventual failure of Joseph's business after his father's decease in 1897 forced the family into smaller and cheaper housing and by the 1901 Census they are living at 62 Milton Street, even though not very far from their former home on Wednesbury Road. Joseph is not given as having any occupation at the time, nor is his 24-year-old son Frank James. Olivia May is then aged 19 and is not listed with an occupation either, so she was possibly running the house which included three younger sisters aged from 14 to 9.

Another ten years on, the 1911 Census reveals that the family has started to break up. Eldest daughter Olivia May has left Walsall altogether and is living in Bloomsbury in London, aged 29, working as a chambermaid in a boarding house. Eldest son, Frank James, has also left, in his case emigrating to Canada where he laboured in Manitoba, Alberta and British Columbia, finally settling in Vancouver. He departed in 1903 on board the S.S. Southwark of the Dominion Line. His father, Joseph Parkes, took passage to join him in Canada in 1907, aboard the S.S. Siberian, ending up in Winnipeg, Manitoba. The story among Joseph's descendants in Vancouver is that he and son Frank were the 'advance guard', the hope being that the other children might in due course follow. Both Frank and Joseph were taking advantage of Canada's 'assisted passages scheme' which gave special rates for male labourers and those in trades like engineering. The sisters could also make use of the scheme if they designated themselves as domestic servants. Joseph's idea was to be able to earn enough to send his children the money so they could sail out to Canada as well. The cost of an assisted passage to Canada at the time was six guineas, which typically meant travelling in 'steerage'.

Joseph Parkes, Olivia's father, outside what is thought to be part of the Manitoba Gypsum Company works in Winnipeg, Manitoba circa 1910 (image courtesy Doug Brock)

Winnipeg in the province of Manitoba is one of the coldest cities in Canada and Joseph soon found that working all year, i.e. through the winter, was very hard. He wrote to his daughter Kathleen that he once managed six weeks in one winter, but his feet, hands, nose and ears all froze. It was therefore best to make enough money in the summer to take you through each winter. In the end, Joseph gained settled work at the Manitoba Gypsum Company Ltd., founded in Winnipeg in 1904 by a Scotsman named William Martin. The company made Plaster of Paris. Initially, Joseph worked in the mill, but later he was managing an office, where he once wryly complained in a letter to Kathleen about the amount of phone work that was involved: 'the blessed thing was going all day'. It impeded him reckoning his books. There was a family cousin already settled in Winnipeg, Mrs. Alice Davis, who was the proprietress of a boarding house at 367 Carlton Street, and it may be that this is how Joseph came to stop in Winnipeg in the first place. In the 1911 Canada Census, she is given as a widow, 46 years of age, with a son and a daughter in their twenties living at the same address. She had emigrated to Canada in 1905. Carlton Street was part of a middle-class neighbourhood with some rather fine multi-storey homes where rooms were often advertised for rent. When Kathleen, Florence and, later, Nora, were planning their journeys to Canada, Joseph suggested her as a first contact for them. This was prior to their making their way to Vancouver, British Columbia, near to where son Frank was by then working. It may well be that Joseph had lodged with Alice at some stage, as he suggested that Nora telegram her when she landed in Canada and that, should she wish to break her journey to the Pacific coast, he would arrange that she stay with cousin Alice. At the time, Joseph was residing on Ashburn Street in Winnipeg, which was just a few blocks away.

Back in Britain, the Census of 1911 has four Parkes children still in Walsall. They all live at 89 Lumley Road, an outer eastern district of the town that was developed for housing in the last years of the nineteenth century. William Summerfield Parkes is then aged 27 and works as a guard on Walsall Corporation Tramways, while sisters Kathleen and Nora are working in the fancy leather trade for which Walsall had long been famous. The youngest of the children, Florence, then aged 19, has no occupation given. The small family unit at Lumley Road did not, however, long survive the date of that spring's Census enumeration. In the May of 1911, Kathleen and Florence sailed to Canada aboard S.S. Lake Manitoba of the Canadian Pacific Line, intent on making for Vancouver in British Columbia to join brother Frank James. Then, exactly a year later, in May 1912, Nora left: on the S.S. Canada, of the Dominion Line, also destined for Vancouver.

This left William as the last one of the family remaining in Walsall (image courtesy Doug Brock). He soon ceased working on Walsall Corporation Tramways and became, instead, a leather worker. Then, in March 1916, he was called up for the war effort, initially joining the Devonshire Regiment, but later transferring to the Duke of Edinburgh's (Wiltshire) Regiment, the 2nd battalion. Sadly, he was killed on active service in France on 15th October 1916, aged just 32, another of the many casualties of his generation. He was serving in France as a member of a Lewis Gun team and his death is recorded on the Thiepval Memorial, but there is no known grave. It seems that Will had always been close to his sister Kathleen, for she mourned his passing well into her later life.

William left his pay and death gratuity to Dora Cockayne, a saddle stitcher in Walsall. She was also 32 years of age and perhaps a 'sweetheart' whom he had met at work. In the 1911 Census, she is recorded as a deaf mute, but was clearly able to work in the leather trade.

We do not know when or why Olivia May decided to leave Walsall for London. The 1911 Census reveals the other occupants of 40 Bloomsbury Street, the boarding house where she resided (image from Google Earth). The proprietress was Mary Price, a widow aged 50. Her 25-year-old son James lived with her and was working as an advertising agent. Another occupant was Elizabeth Mytton, a niece of Mary Price, who was aged 29. Olivia was also 29 at the time and it is possible that the two became friends, even though Olivia was ostensibly a servant. The Bloomsbury house may offer a clue as to how Olivia came to arrive in Ventnor in 1919, for in the 1921 Census, Mary Price and her son James are listed as living in Southsea, Portsmouth, Mary with no occupation given, but James entered as advertising manager for a local drapery and furnishing emporium. As their chambermaid in Bloomsbury, Olivia had possibly moved down with her. Mary's son James, a sergeant in the Welsh Guards during the war, was discharged from duty in April 1919, which may have been the point at which the move down from Bloomsbury was made.

40 Bloomsbury Street

Olivia's time in London does seem to have left a lasting impression on her. One of the other residents at 40, Bloomsbury Street in the spring of 1911 was the renowned Australian-born music hall artiste and acrobat dancer who went by the stage name 'Saharet'. She was born Paulina Clarissa Molony (1878-1964) and became internationally famous, performing in Europe and on Broadway as well as across the USA. The height of her career was between around 1905 and 1914, in other words, coinciding with the time that Olivia figures as a live-in servant at 40, Bloomsbury Street in the 1911 Census. On September 20th 1911, 'Saharet' was performing alongside Sarah Bernhardt at the Coliseum in London, the New York magazine Variety subsequently recording how the fashionable audience yelled itself frantic.

Whether encouraged by 'Saharet', or in imitation of her, Olivia developed a passion for dancing (Saharet image, left, from The Tatler 20/9/1911, courtesy Mary Evans Picture Library). We know this from photos of her at the time, and from references she made later in life about her dancing dress and shoes. Servants who lived in their establishments worked long hours and would have had little time for such a pursuit. Olivia may thus have pursued her interest either before or after the time when she was recorded as a chambermaid in Bloomsbury in 1911. According to the grandson of Kathleen (the younger sister in Vancouver), Olivia was known to have been in theatre, and the two photos opposite and those overleaf rather confirm this. Kathleen also left a memo stating that the reason Olivia never followed her other sisters to Canada was because she had been 'stage-struck' in London. Perhaps she became involved in some way with 'Saharet', either as a personal maid, or else in her shows. Saharet, moreover, was often described in the press as 'Madame Saharet', a practice that Olivia was to copy in Ventnor. 'Saharet' was well-known, too, as a supporter of women's suffrage, insisting on a woman chauffeur on tour. Olivia's later obstinacy may have taken cue from her.

The dates of these two photos of Olivia are unknown, but a fair guess is that it is when she was in her twenties, in other words circa 1900-1910. They accord with her family's observation that Olivia had been in the theatre while in London. (images courtesy of Blake's Longshoreman's Museum, Ventnor)

With best wishes
Your loving sister
Cissy 1911.

Portrait by Gyde. Aberystwyth.

Above and opposite, two fine studio portraits of Olivia, one dated 1911, and taken by Edward Gyde, a photographer in Pier Street, Aberystwyth, the other also taken in Aberystwyth, probably at the same time, but by Pickford, an associate of Gyde. Both pictures belonged to Olivia's younger sister, Kathleen, and passed down to her grandson and great granddaughter. It may be that Olivia went to the Welsh resort that year as part of a theatre act, or that she even went with 'Saharet'. The style of both photographs is certainly consistent with Olivia having developed some sort of stage presence. The name 'Cissy' in the photo above was the one used for Olivia within the family (images courtesy Lauren Johnstone and Doug Brock).

With best wishes
from :—
Cissy Parkes.

This close image shows the Hut in the early 1900s when it had been taken over by the Blakes, a family of Ventnor Longshoremen. They dispensed with the veranda and extended the beach-facing elevation right to the edge, to give a larger floor area. The hut also now had double doors.
(VHC – Fay Brown Collection)

THE HISTORY OF THE OLD BOATHOUSE

The Undercliff Swimming Club was the body that first alighted on the idea of a swimming hut in Myrtle Bay. Swimming off Ventnor beach was heavily regulated, separating men from women, requiring the hire of a bathing machine, an attendant, and a costume. On sunny and calm days in season, the sea there could get quite crowded. There were also canoes, rowing boats and sail-boats that could be hired for use in and around the bay. It was thus quite understandable that an amateur club whose members were experienced and some perhaps competition swimmers might seek out a more open stretch of water. They found it in Myrtle Bay which in the early 1880s enjoyed a largely sandy beach. A beach hut was thus constructed for their use near the very base of the cliffs and also close to the steps giving access down from the clifftop. The Club had both men and women members and, at times, welcomed individuals from other clubs. Learners were also taught to swim. On one occasion, a woman from the Portsmouth Club is recorded as saving two lives from drowning.

Unfortunately, this first hut washed away in a winter storm of 1886, and the Swimming Club, observing the work that was taking place in building Ventnor's pier in the late 1880s, decided to approach Trehearne's, the company working on it, to erect a hut for them in Myrtle Bay, set on piles. The hope was that such a design would protect it from storms. In May 1887, the Mercury reported that work had started on positioning piles for the Swimming Club's new changing room. The Hut ultimately had a veranda along its front, while access up to it from the shore was via a hinged ladder that was pulled down by a hooked pole, the pole kept hidden so that there could be no unauthorised entry.

The Undercliff Swimming Club had become defunct around 1900 and the Hut was bought by Blakes Longshoremen for boat and gear storage in winter, after modifications to its structure (see picture caption opposite). About 1920, Blakes sold the Hut and it was used as a kind of holiday bungalow by various individuals. We do not yet know who any of them were, but we do know that Ventnor Council, in October 1926, ordered proceedings to be brought against the Hut's owner for obstructing the Local Medical Officer of Health in making an inspection as part of performing his duties under the 1925 Housing Act. It is possible that these proceedings arose because the Hut was being rented out as a holiday home at the time, even though it was without a water supply or sanitation. Finally, around 1929 or 1930, Miss Parkes bought the Hut and, within a year or two, had made it her permanent home before the War. It was here that she lived in semi-isolation for some 28 or 29 years, with just a brief absence in the later years of War, following her court conviction of June 1942.

Over the following years, Olivia Parkes became more and more an object of curiosity, especially for holidaymakers. Whereas in the 1930s, such an isolated dwelling place would not have excited a great deal in the way of comment, by the late 1940s and 1950s much the opposite was true. Not only was it the case that she was now a woman getting to her seventies, but she lived in the hut all year round. And as everyone who peered down at it from the cliff, or descended the steps to the shore could see, it was far from watertight by this time. How could anyone of that age survive bitter winter weather, winds blowing in off the sea from the east straight from Siberia. How could she keep warm outside of the summer months? How could she ensure a supply of water? How did she get supplies of paraffin for cooking and lighting up those precarious steps?

The Old Boathouse around 1950, the steps still with their handrail, but with clear signs of roof damage and no longer any handrail to the platform outside the double doors. The tide is low and the beach plainly boulder-strewn, making walking along it in either direction hazardous (VHC- Elaine Farrant deposit).

Local inhabitants often noted that Miss Parkes seemed to be in good health. And this remained the case right up to the time that she moved to a flat on the High Street late in 1958. Perhaps it was all those piles of newspapers she had accumulated that provided rudimentary insulation from cold winds? For food, she appeared to live a lot of the time on tinned produce which meant that the lack of a refrigerator was rarely a problem. Tinned food, today, is now regarded as far more nutritious than most 'ready-made' or 'instant' meals, so perhaps this helped maintain her health. Several times a day, she would climb the steps to the Boathouse, laden with water or paraffin. She walked west to Flowers Brook along the beach and back to get water and to wash her things. The paraffin had to be fetched from town. She was, in other words, far from what once was described as a 'couch potato'. She had no television to sit and watch for hours on end. She would walk up into the town on most days with a shopping bag, sometimes just to buy a newspaper, but otherwise to buy daily supplies from the shops in Pier Street. The plethora of health commentators in the lifestyle sections of today's Sunday papers would probably look at Olivia's daily routine and see it now as a recipe for long life. In fact, living hidden away in her 'eyrie', having limited contact with others, would have reduced her chances of picking up respiratory infections, particularly in winter. One hundred years before, of course, Ventnor in winter had often been full of chesty invalids sleeping out on balconies in the raw air, with just a canvas sheet to protect them from rain and wind. We now know that exposure to cold can stimulate the immune system, so perhaps Olivia was doing just that whilst continuing to live in the Old Boathouse. Maybe this was another clue to her apparent good health, even though she would largely have been unaware of it.

Olivia just outside the double doors of the Old Boathouse in the mid-1950s. The signs of rotting timber are yet more apparent in this close-up. It is remarkable that she never seems to have had a serious fall going up and down those unrailed wooden steps. This particular image soon became iconic of Olivia's later life. Some observers thought her a bit crazed (VHC – Gill Lloyd deposit).

One of the most legitimate concerns over Britannia's Hut by the 1950s was the state of decay of some of the oak piles, very clearly visible in this image. It appears that some or all of them had at some point been encased in concrete bases as a safety measure against violent storm waves. But this would likely have quickened the pace at which these timbers rotted, taking longer to dry out than would otherwise have been the case when exposed to the air. (VHC – Elaine Farrant deposit)

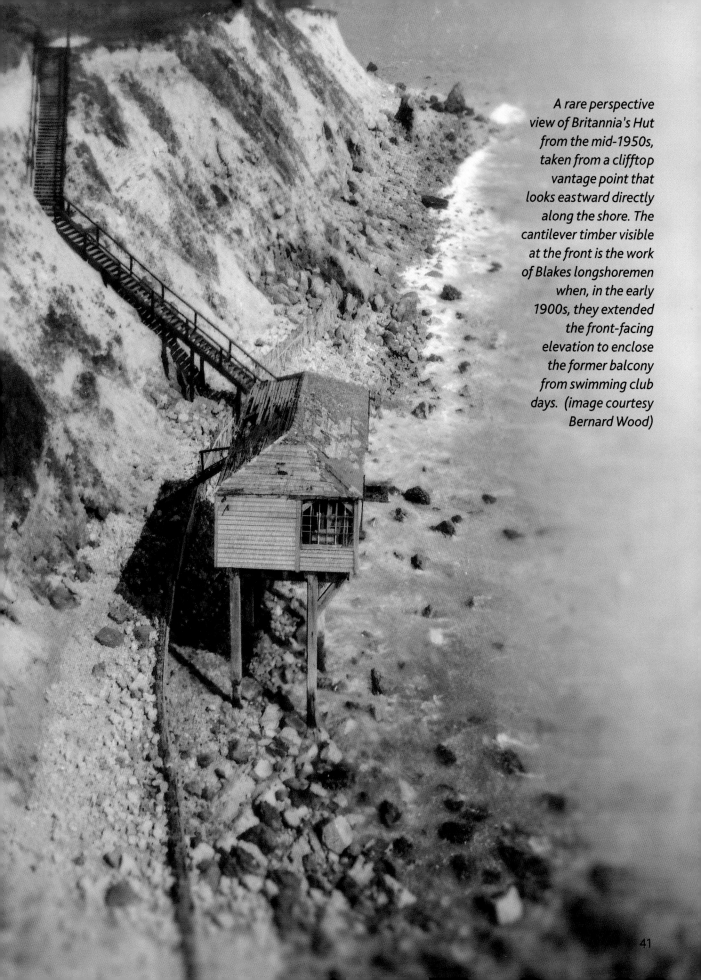

A rare perspective view of Britannia's Hut from the mid-1950s, taken from a clifftop vantage point that looks eastward directly along the shore. The cantilever timber visible at the front is the work of Blakes longshoremen when, in the early 1900s, they extended the front-facing elevation to enclose the former balcony from swimming club days. (image courtesy Bernard Wood)

The Hut's terrible state of devastation is very apparent from this late-1950s image. Around half of the rear roof area has now gone. The large canvas sheet that Olivia had used to shield the inside from the rain would have been wholly inadequate to the task (VHC – Elaine Farrant deposit).

A DEMOLITION ORDER

In the early post-war years, local councils across the United Kingdom had powers to condemn habitations that were damp or insanitary. In major urban areas, this resulted in large-scale clearance of what were described as slums. Whole swathes of nineteenth-century terrace housing were swept away, to be replaced by high rise flats. What many do not also register is that a not dissimilar policy was operated in the countryside, whereby all manner of rural cottages, ancient as well as more recent, typically thatched, and with nothing but an earth closet and a well or stream for fresh water, were summarily condemned as unfit for habitation and torn down. In December 1954, Ventnor Council made a demolition order against the Old Boathouse in Myrtle Bay as unfit for habitation. This was plainly not a case of a dilapidated farm cottage, but it fell into much the same category. Olivia Parkes, however, would have none of it and refused to come to court to represent her case. This was despite offers of alternative accommodation. Her plight and her determination to remain in her home seems to have struck a chord with quite an array of townspeople. The local newspaper, the Mercury, became the conduit for various of these dissenting voices. A local carpenter, Mr. Gilbert, questioned why the Council had made no effort to stop the damage that was woefully done by children throwing stones at the Boathouse, to the extent that on one occasion the occupier had been injured. He suggested that the Council organise a repair scheme. He also wondered whether the Council had powers to force the demolition of a structure that was below the high water mark. He further suggested that a strong wire mesh screen could be fixed a short distance above the roof of the boathouse to prevent it being further vandalised by children.

This prompted a lengthy piece from a local 'housewife', name and address not supplied. She wrote as 'another woman', criticising the reports in the County Press and in the Mercury that neither newspaper had given thought or space to the idea that the damaged boathouse might be repaired. She questioned why the occupier should become an extra burden on the local Housing Committee, when there was an obvious solution to hand. And why had nothing been done to bring to book the damage to the building caused by local children. None had been charged for their misdemeanours, let alone charged to pay for the damage. The 'housewife' rehearsed the familiar adage that 'an Englishman's home was his castle'. Miss Parkes owned this building. She had lived there over many years. She did not want to leave. The Council, in the housewife's view, had gone about this matter in the wrong way.

There was no further movement for almost four more years to force Miss Parkes out of the Old Boathouse, suggesting that the community at large had generated wider sympathy with this gallant defence of an elderly woman's rights, eschewing any notion that a woman had lesser rights than any man. It seems that there was also some ambiguity over the issue within the Council. Mr S.G. Conbeer, a Labour Party councillor, remarked that since the lady was the owner of the property and was apparently in perfectly good health, they faced a very difficult situation. Slow persuasion might be a better approach than the use of force.

Olivia slowly climbing the steps to her hut, with two bags, one in either hand, in the very last years of her life at the boathouse (image courtesy John Howell)

RECALLED TO MODERN LIFE

It is the morning of Friday 31st October 1958 and Olivia Parkes, aged 76, sits in the kitchen of her first-floor flat in the centre of Ventnor after her first night away from the Old Boathouse in Myrtle Bay, her home for almost three decades. She is warmed by two oil stoves that the Council has provided. And as she sits in the kitchen becoming accustomed to her strange new environment, three men are busy fitting a two-burner gas ring. She had slept the night in a bed provided by the Council and they had also provided her with food.

The image shows number 47, High Street, Ventnor, on the corner of the junction with Spring Hill to the left. It was once commonly known as Chaplin's Corner. The image dates from shortly before this entire range of buildings fell to the demolition ball about 1970. (VHC – M. Vine deposit)

Olivia moved here after she was ejected from the Old Boathouse at the end of October 1958. She was in the first-floor flat, with the three false window arches on the left, a bay window in the centre and then three conventional windows on the right, above the High Street proper. Entrance to the flat (as well as to the one above) was via the small doorway at the building's extreme left. There were some stairs for Olivia to climb, but nothing to compare to the steps at her former home.

It was in July of 1958 that Ventnor Council finally took the formal decision to act on its view of four years earlier that the Old Boathouse was not fit for human habitation. The roof had long ceased to be watertight, especially on the landward side, successive cohorts of children, young and old, having continued to wreck it with stones. The glazing in the boathouse windows had all gone, its double doors were rotting, as were the eight massive oak piles that the boathouse had stood upon since it was erected in the late 1880s. All the piles were very seriously eroded at their base and there was real anxiety that one or more of them could fail in a severe winter storm, possibly resulting in the entire structure collapsing into the sea.

The Council had still continued to hope that they could get Olivia to move out by gentle persuasion and, in particular, by offering her a flat in the town. The matter was kept as quiet as possible to try to avoid alarm. However, when it became plain that Olivia would not move out voluntarily, it was decided to obtain an 'ejectment order'. There was still not unanimity in the Council's decision. There were some members who remained of the view that she should be left alone, as her health seemed none the worse for living in such increasingly dilapidated conditions. Ultimately, though, an application for ejectment was made.

The local police force had the task of carrying out the order and she was quietly intercepted while out shopping on the afternoon of October 30th and taken to the police station. After various formalities, she was then taken to the flat set aside for her at 47 High Street by the bottom of Spring Hill. At the time, it was above Fletcher's greengrocer shop.

A close-up of the entrance to the flat above 47 High Street when Fletcher's grocery store was in place below. The doorway is clearly visible to the right of the decorative stone pillar. (VHC – Fay Brown Collection)

Olivia had been shown it previously, at the time when there was hope that she would move out of the boathouse voluntarily. She then described it as 'very peculiar' and 'prehistoric', remarks that possibly related more to the external appearance of the building in which the flat was situated: it had a late-nineteenth century institutional façade, perhaps reminding her of some of Walsall's public buildings from her childhood. However, this verdict was no longer of any relevance.

Later that day, Council workmen, supervised by the Town Clerk and the Town Surveyor, went to the boathouse and began to bundle up her many belongings, securing them with rope and then sliding them to the shore on ladders, prior to Bert Mew, a local haulier, delivering them to her flat the next morning. Bert had been the one who moved Miss Parkes's effects from her Pier Street shop to the Boathouse 29 years before. Once they had finished, the workmen took away the precarious steps up to the boathouse and a plank was nailed across the double doors to deter anyone who tried scaling the piles and entering inside. By the next day, there could be no mistaking that the structure was now formally derelict, wholly at the mercy of rain, wind and sea. Its fate was finally sealed when, a few months later, in February 1959, the Council took the decision to get Blakes Longshoremen to dismantle it on the grounds of it being a danger to the public. By that summer, it was gone.

Myrtle Bay in summer 1959, half of 'Britannia's Hut' already dismantled, with just three of the oak piles left and a few of the joists. It was an era when health and safety rules were not what they are now. There is no scaffolding and just one ladder (image courtesy Blake's Longshoreman's Museum).

Back in her new home, with gas now laid on, with electric light and running water, Olivia remains slightly dazed at the event of her move. She admitted to a news reporter that 'one must get out of a rut some time, I suppose'. But she had been given no opportunity to sort and pack up her things, so they now surround her in the bundles put together by the Council workmen the day before. She cannot find her teapot, her toothbrush or her rolling pin. She can find only some of her clothes. Her feet are cold wearing just the canvas shoes she had on when the policeman intercepted her in the town. Jim Blake, the longshoreman who knew Olivia quite well, recalled that she appeared most worried by not being able to find her dancing dress or her dancing shoes, things she would have worn while living in London before the Great War.

The reporter goes on to ask her whether she misses living right by the sea. Her snapped response was that she had 'no love for that'; but she did miss the sea air and her 'little corner'. She thought that living over a greengrocer would have decided advantages (this from someone who years back sold fruit on the beach and cliffs, often sourced from the slightly over-ripe stock of the local grocers). It was handy, too, to have other shops close by and there was now gas to cook her food. Above all, she did not have to trek along the shore to fetch fresh water (from Flowers Brook). It had lately become a 'very heavy job' she observed. Finally, a reporter enquired if she went out on her first day in the flat. Apparently, she walked down to the 'promenade' (esplanade) and had a pot of tea which she enjoyed very much (presumably a little compensation for not being able to find her teapot).

Olivia on Ventnor Esplanade one summer, probably in the mid-1950s, before her move to 47 High Street on 31st October 1958. It is without a doubt the 1950s, demonstrated by the two cars: a Standard 8 in the centre and a Morris Minor just in view to the left (Image courtesy Erich Frank Wheeler)

One of the startling things about the weeks running up to Olivia's ejection from the boathouse is the way the news of it (and of her plight, generally) steadily permeated across the media, the newspaper media in the first instance (including national news-papers) and subsequently over tele-vision, both the BBC and ITV.

Miss Parkes Appears On Television

People in the town who are able to receive an ITV picture were surprised to see Miss Olivia Parkes, of Myrtle Bay, featured in the programme " Southern Affairs," on Sunday afternoon. Cyril Ray, introducing the feature, commencing with a quip on the old adage : " There was an old woman . . ."

Viewers were taken to the cliff-top, and the hut in the bay could clearly be seen. The battered, holed roof was particularly clear.

In its issue of 17th October 1958, the *Mercury* (VHC) related how people in the town had been surprised to see Miss Olivia Parkes of Myrtle Bay feature on the 'Southern Affairs' tv programme on the preceding Sunday afternoon. Viewers who could receive Southern Television were taken to the cliff-top where the hut in Myrtle Bay could clearly be seen on screen, including its battered and holed roof, with Miss Parkes relating to the film reporter how she had once run a chocolate shop in the town. When asked about the eviction notice issued to her, she asserted that she could not be turned out of her own place. It was boys who had made it look disreputable by smashing the roof with stones. Even so, she thought the boathouse 'was a credit to her', a comment that must have rather non-plussed the reporter, given its state of dilapidation.

On the 31st October 1958 following, the *Mercury* reported on a second television appearance, but this time with the BBC. The programme 'Tonight', fronted by Cliff Michelmore (incidentally a native of the Island from Cowes) showed a film interview with Miss Parkes, made by Trevor Philpot. She told him how she had lived in the Boathouse for 38 years and would soon be 77 years of age. In fact, she had lived there for 28 not 38 years, but it was still a long time, and the wider point clearly stood. She was not frightened living there. She conceded that the council had offered her a place in an old folk's home, or else a flat. But she did not want to leave. Mr. Philpot was at pains to point out that he thought the Ventnor Council was both reasonable and compassionate. The Housing Committee chairman (Mrs. Ingram) and the Town Clerk (Mr. Davies) were concerned that the boathouse was unfit and dangerous. They worried that it could break up in a severe gale. They were also concerned that Miss Parkes had no light or water and had to trail up into the town most days. It was already the case that the local longshoremen and the local police were checking on her if she had not been seen about, though rarely would any of them manage to gain admittance. It had also been the case, for some time, that there were other locals who gave Olivia practical help and sustenance. She was not in any way a figure who was oppressed across the board and, as has been seen, officialdom was not invariably impatient with her chosen mode of living.

Several months earlier than either of the television features, Miss Parkes's story became a subject for a column in the Daily Mail of Wednesday 20th August 1958. A large grainy image of the boathouse was presented to readers, with Miss Parkes standing on the rotting planking outside the double doors, the precarious wooden steps down to the shore clearly visible. The journalist remarked how 'we all have our own ideas of happiness', but none compared to the home shown in the tiny cove in the picture: 'a ramshackle hut, once a boathouse, perched 15 ft above the rocks'. He related how the local council had repeatedly offered to find her a good home in the nearby town, but Miss Parkes had refused. He went on to remark how, during the war, when the Island was fortified, Miss Parkes had to vacate the hut. He wrote that she 'had to go [to] the north of England'. Eventually, she was allowed to return, walking most of the way back, so it was claimed.

As we indeed know, Olivia was forced to leave the Old Boathouse after June 1942, but there is no corroborative evidence as to where she went. She had a cousin on her mother's side, Elsie Marsh, who lived in Walsall, and it is possible that this is where she went. In 1939, Elsie is recorded as being at 49 Tasker Street in the town, running a boarding house. Olivia's sister in Vancouver, Kathleen, kept in correspondence with Elsie right up to the 1950s, suggesting, in other words, that the cousins were all close at one time. Ultimately, though, it is a guessing game. In Ventnor, no record survives of Olivia for the later part of the war.

Olivia was buried in an unmarked grave, seen here marked by daffodils. It is close to the cemetery chapel and next to William John Knight, a notable Ventnor tradesman (image courtesy Robert Trowbridge).

DEATH AND FUNERAL

Olivia Parkes was found dead at her Flat, 47, High Street, Ventnor, on 19th January 1962. She had turned 80 years old the preceding November. It is not known if she actually died that day as she lived alone. Mrs W. Gee, who helped care for Olivia in her final three years, found the body. The Gees were fruiterers and florists in Ventnor over many years and were long acquainted with Olivia.

The Isle of Wight Mercury, dated 26th January 1962, had her death as its main headline, with the rather poignant sub-title: 'Alone she lived; alone she died'. It reported that P.C. Riggs had found her dead, but this was not strictly correct. He was called in after Mrs Gee had discovered her. The Mercury observed that her health had deteriorated in the last few years. It offered readers a summary of Olivia's life (not wholly accurate) since the time she had arrived in Ventnor some forty or so years before. It also described her as 'one of Ventnor's best-known characters'. There was a post-mortem but not an inquest. The cause of death was revealed as a 'Subarachnoid Haemorrhage' and 'Broncho-pneumonia'.

A funeral was held at Ventnor Cemetery on Tuesday 30th January. There were twelve in attendance. The mourners were: Mr and Mrs A. Whitehouse who had known Miss Parkes's family in Walsall, Mr and Mrs W. Gee, Mrs Jack Spencer, Mesdames K. Attwaters and H. Jones, and Mr. J. Parsons. Mrs F.E. Ingram represented the Town Council. Messrs R. Wearing and L.F. Rodaway also attended. Mr Wearing was editor of the Mercury. Interment took place in a grave near the cemetery chapel. The Council had made efforts to contact Miss Parkes's two surviving sisters who were still living in Vancouver.

Olivia left no Will but Administration was granted to Noel John Wade, solicitor attorney for sisters Florence Mabel Parkes and Kathleen Matilda Brown (née Parkes), both living in Vancouver. The estate was valued at £397.13s.9d. In today's money, that would amount to around £10,000, a remarkable sum given Olivia's life story. Some of this may have derived from a legacy or an annuity. It would have paid for her funeral and other expenses.

The Isle of Wight County Press and the Isle of Wight Mercury each reported on Olivia's funeral, and one might have thought that her death would bring her story to a close. But it did not. From time to time, letters would appear in newspapers (national as well as local), enquiring about the lady who once lived in the Old Boathouse at Myrtle Bay. These letters would then get answered, quite often with inaccuracies in them, as well as with an element of wishful thinking. Even 60 years after her death, Olivia remains a very live historical figure, increasingly enigmatic in an age where there is far greater sensitivity towards individuals who do not conform to prescribed social norms. In 2023, Arts Council England funded a project: Olivia Parkes, Britannia, the old lady of the sea, led by Teresa Grimaldi and Sarah Vardy, both from Ventnor. It encompassed the making of an animated film and 'zine' around the 'outsider' life of Olivia Parkes who, as has been recounted, lived for many years 'off-grid' in a boathouse on stilts on the sea shore. The project's wider aim was to use Olivia's story to help explore the mental health and physical well-being of the way unconventional people are treated in society in present times. In this respect, the project sought to offer creative opportunities for people in the present community who had had to combat a lack of inclusivity and experienced degrees of marginalisation in their lives. The results of the 'Olivia' project were showcased at the Ventnor Fringe Festival in July 2023 and later re-exhibited at Quay Arts, Newport Harbour.

For all such present-day perspectives on Olivia, though, it is worth bearing in mind that one hundred years ago, Ventnor had quite a number of 'eccentric' or 'oddball' characters, people who did not really fit the 'norm' in some way. There was once a resident nicknamed 'Gandhi' (nobody seems to know why he was so named) who lived at the bottom of Longdown steps between the wars. His real name was Stuart Whildey. He once delivered bread around the town – on foot and with a large basket. Where the pavements were narrow, he would often just barge people out of the way. The local schoolkids would often taunt him verbally outside his home, whereupon he would react in angry fashion, chasing them away with his stick.

Another yet stranger character was 'Holy Joe'. His real name was Alexander Gray and he seems to have turned up in Ventnor in the 1890s. His place of dwelling had all the eccentricities associated with Olivia. In summer, it was a natural bower among trees and bushes in Steephill Cove, or else a shelter near La Falaise on the Western Cliffs. In winter, he found refuge in a cave on the Steephill Castle estate. The nickname 'Holy Joe' derived from his habit of offering loud evangelising street sermons, at times haranguing passers-by about the dangers of hellfire and damnation. A favoured location was along the Esplanade, sometimes on the steps of one of the smart boarding houses. He survived in part on the charity of townsfolk. If he smelt a dinner cooking, he would sometimes enter the house, sit down, and wait to be fed. It was not unknown, either, for him to enter a café, order a meal, and then refuse to pay. The standard response was that 'the Lord would provide'. In August 1909, he was convicted by magistrates in absentia for disorderly conduct in public places and fined, or face three weeks in prison. However, 'Holy Joe' had another side to him. He had his portrait taken and then got it reproduced on postcards which he proceeded to sell to visitors. Some of the parallels with Olivia's life-story are, in parts, uncanny.

A little westward from Myrtle Bay, at Steephill Cove, Olivia even had a neighbour or, perhaps, fellow 'recluse'. He was a man by the name of Jock Howard. He lived in a beach hut there between about 1940 and 1945 and was mainly looked after by the Wheeler family, the local longshoremen. He typically wore a Breton cap, spending much of each day just shuffling about. He made good use of the old public toilet that was near the beach, plainly one up on Olivia who had no water or sanitation at the Old Boathouse.

Steephill Cove, in a view taken from the inter-war years. Jock Howard, a loner like Olivia, spent most of the years of the Second World War living in a beach hut here (image courtesy Digweed family archive).

Alexander Gray in preaching mode, Holy Bible in hand, posing for Digweed & Co., the local Ventnor photographer (Digweed family archive).

English Bay in Vancouver one fine August day circa 1920, crowded with beach-goers and bathers (Vancouverarchives.ca). Sometimes known as Vancouver's first beach, it was the location of the city's first lifeguard who taught many early residents to swim. There is a fine promenade to the right. The Parkes family would have spent time here, especially Kathleen with her two young daughters.

OLIVIA'S FAMILY IN VANCOUVER, BRITISH COLUMBIA

We can try and offer some sort of Coda to Olivia's life in terms of the lives of her father and her four other surviving siblings from whom she had been separated for more than fifty years. Four of the siblings emigrated to Canada, as previously recounted.

Frank James was the first, in 1903, where he ultimately settled in Vancouver, working as a logger. He never married and died in Vancouver in 1956. He is pictured here in Britain around 1900, first on the left (image courtesy Doug Brock), waiting for a train on a country station somewhere on the Great Western Railway. It was perhaps on a Sunday outing.

Frank's sister, Kathleen Matilda, arrived in Vancouver in 1911 and eventually married Robert Hunter Brown, a Scot who had emigrated to Canada in 1906 and a carpenter by trade. Their wedding was actually held in Dundee, Scotland, in February 1917, for Robert Brown was in the Canadian 29th Infantry Battalion (the legendary 'Tobin's Tigers') during the Great War, serving in France from September 1915.

Kathleen had sailed back to Britain for the marriage ceremony, for she is recorded as then living at the home of Robert's parents in Dundee. Kathleen returned to Canada later that year, but it proved to be a testing passage, as the liner was hit by a German torpedo not long out of port. The story passed down through her family is that the vessel's crew managed to effect repairs and, with the help of the pumps, was able to complete the transatlantic voyage. The identity of the liner has not been found, but there was an Allan Line ship, the Virginian, that sustained a torpedo hit off Tory Island on 21st August 1917 as it left Lough Swilly on Ireland's north coast, en route from Liverpool to Montreal. The liner withdrew back into Lough Swilly for the crew to make temporary repairs and then returned to Liverpool, going into dry dock for three months, and not sailing for Canada again until early December. Husband Robert did not return to Canada from his war service until the summer of 1919. Robert and Kathleen Brown then went on to have two daughters, with Kathleen herself living on in Vancouver well into her nineties (image courtesy Doug Brock).

Younger sister Nora (pictured centre, courtesy Doug Brock) arrived in Vancouver in 1912 and in 1915 married Edward Lee Marler, a sawyer by trade. They had two children, the first dying as an infant and Nora herself sadly dying in a TB sanatorium in Tranquille, British Columbia in 1928 in her late thirties. Florence, the youngest of all the siblings, had arrived in 1911 with sister Kathleen and died unmarried in Vancouver in 1967.

The children's father, Joseph Parkes, had emigrated to Canada in 1907, as previously described, ostensibly to join son Frank. He had departed from Liverpool in June that year, destination Halifax, Nova Scotia. For much of the next four or five years, he was in Winnipeg, as we know, working for the Manitoba Gypsum Co. Ltd. Sometime in late 1912, he became ill and moved to Vancouver to be close to his son and daughters. It is clear from surviving correspondence that Joseph's employer thought highly of him, for he was offered half pay for a set period, daughter Kathleen eventually being sent a cheque for 180 dollars on her father's behalf. This would be about 6,000 dollars in today's values, a clear measure of Joseph's business competence and certainly confounding some of the assertions made 10 years before at his bankruptcy hearing. Some time in the early spring of 1913, Joseph was admitted to the newly-built Vancouver General Hospital and, very sadly, passed away there on 27th May 1913, aged 60. He was buried by his family in Mountain View Cemetery. It was a sad end to a life that had started so well: marrying at the young age of 23, fathering 6 children and a successful Walsall ironfounder.

What remains remarkable is how far the Parkes family unit managed, over a period of years, to re-establish itself thousands of miles away in one of the dominions, in spite of all the life traumas in Walsall. Three of the men, Frank James and his two new brothers-in-law, were initially working in Vancouver's thriving timber trade and that is probably how they all met originally. The core of the town grew around the site of the Hastings Mill and the seaport. Logging and the timber trades provided the basis of Vancouver's early prosperity, especially after the Canadian Pacific Railway opened its transcontinental terminus in Vancouver in 1886. Emigrants from Britain and later from Europe were soon feeding the rising demand for labour in the colony, its population growing rapidly from under 14,000 in 1891 to 117,000 in 1921 and then 246,000 by 1931. The Parkes siblings were eventually able to find relative financial security in Vancouver and to live reasonably comfortable lives, as do their direct descendants to this day.

Hastings Street, Vancouver, the view from Hamilton St. towards Homer St., circa 1910. This was quite close to where the Parkes siblings lived for a time on Helmcken St., as well as near to where some of them worked (image courtesy Vancouverarchives.ca).

It is very hard, well into the twenty-first century, for us to grasp the magnitude of a decision to emigrate to North America in the early 1900s, so accustomed as we are today to foreign travel. The transatlantic crossing was then all of seven days and sometimes many more, depending on the size of the vessel and the route that it took. This was followed by a four-day journey by rail to the Canadian province of British Columbia in the Pacific North-West, on the other side of the North American continent, though some emigrants would break that journey, especially if they had relations already in Canada. The Parkes siblings were all in their twenties when they emigrated and probably viewed it in part as an adventure, but still with the trepidation of a journey into the unknown.

What they eventually found in Vancouver was a settlement that was not all that different in size from the Walsall where they had lived since birth. Nor was the Vancouver climate that different from whence they came. Classified as moderate oceanic, it had rather less cold but wetter winters, and summers that were warm and dry rather than hot, the colony 's weather always tempered by the Pacific Ocean air. However, the face of Vancouver, that is as a place in which to live, would have been a revelation. Situated between the Pacific Ocean and the Rockies, with its rugged landscapes, lakes, forests and beaches, it bore little comparison to the English Midlands. Its rectilinear street grid and wide avenues were poles apart from the sometimes narrow, winding and densely packed streets of Walsall. The buildings themselves were nearly all different, too, invariably constructed of wood, many just single or two-storeyed, other than in the central thoroughfares. Timber was in plentiful supply and cheap in the Pacific Northwest. It was also a staple and growing export. The timber trade, in turn, gave many newly-arrived male emigrants employment, as we have seen.

We know from an exchange of letters between Kathleen and her father in 1911 that she and her younger sister Florence both liked the country after their arrival in Montreal. Joseph wondered in reply how they enjoyed the passage and whether they proved 'good sailors'. When Nora was preparing to leave Walsall for Canada in the following spring of 1912, he wrote again to Kathleen, telling her to re-assure her younger sister not to worry about the 'Titanic' which hit an iceberg that April and sank. He felt certain that it would be a lesson to ship's captains and make them more careful. He also hoped the three sisters, once settled would do well in their new country.

There was, in fact, a growing range of employment opportunities for female emigrant arrivals in Canada. Kathleen Parkes, for example, quickly found work as one of the pioneer telephone exchange operators with the British Columbia Telephone Company. This would have been a very novel role in women's employment and Kathleen would have had little difficulty with the surnames of the telephone subscribers, for they were then mostly English, Welsh or Scottish. It would have seemed almost like home from home.

Her younger sister Nora found employment with the recently formed Empress Manufacturing Company, a maker of jams, jellies, sauces baking powder etc., with its 'moderne' factory erected at the junction of Helmcken Street and Homer Street in 1909 (Google images). It was one of a number of early successful food supply companies in the colony, with 'Empress' quickly adopted as a brand label. Sister Florence also found employment there, as a labeller. At different times over the next thirty or so years, both Kathleen and Florence seem to have had semi-continuous associations with the company, taking on a variety of work roles, especially jam-making. Even Robert Brown, Kathleen's husband, was employed there at one time: as a warehouseman.

232-240 Union Street, Vancouver, the place where the Parkes family lived around 1911-1913, the picture dating from about 1960.
The building was demolished in the late 1960s to effect road improvements (image courtesy Vancouverarchives.ca).

It is quite difficult to trace where new emigrant arrivals lived in their first years. It depended where they happened to find work. If it was regular and full-time, the likelihood is that they put down roots quite soon. But if it was irregular or seasonal, they would move from place to place. We do know, however, that around the time that Kathleen, Florence and Nora arrived in Vancouver, most of the family were living at 232 Union Street, in what is now part of downtown. They occupied one of a group of four three-storey weatherboard houses that had been constructed in 1904. It was here, too, that Joseph, the sisters' father, was living about the end of 1912, having moved there from Winnipeg owing to illness.

By 1917, Henderson's Vancouver Directory shows that Florence was living at 1152 7th Avenue West in the district of Fairview. In April 1917, when Robert Brown assigned some of his army pay to his new wife Kathleen, her address in Vancouver was also given as 1152 7th Avenue West. In 1920, sister Florence subsequently shows up at 1148 7th Avenue West, as does Robert Hunter Brown, Kathleen's husband, by then out of the Canadian Army. Today, this last property appears on the local heritage register, a rather fine-looking weather-board home that has probably been much renewed in subsequent years, but still has sufficient of it that is original to qualify as a heritage building. Both Florence and Robert were then listed as working at the Empress Manufacturing Company at the time. Kathleen, Robert's wife, was plainly also at 1148, but not listed as employed on account of being an expectant mother.

By the date of the 1921 Canada Census, most of the Parkes family had come together to live at 543 Helmcken Street in what is now downtown Vancouver, but was then a largely working-class district not far from the big railway yards and from the sawmills and seaport.

Some of the two-storey timber houses around 513 Helmcken Street today, not far from where the Parkes family lived at number 543 in 1921. Most of the dwellings are still on narrow lots that sit very tightly together. The street is now largely high-rise blocks of mixed business and residential use. (image from Google Earth)

By the mid-1920s, most of the family had moved yet again, this time out to 2823 Pender Street East, a more salubrious district of Vancouver, with Kathleen residing there until her death in 1981, though widowed since her husband's death in 1940. Frank Parkes lived with sister Kathleen for some years.

2823 Pender Street East was a mail-order house from T. Eaton. Kathleen's husband, Robert Brown, a skilled carpenter, erected it. Obtaining homes by mail-order was common in North America in the early half of the twentieth century. There was an enormous range of designs from which to choose. This one was the 'Jenny' model. (image courtesy Doug Brock)

This is a view of Pender Street East, Vancouver, today. Even though the image is modern, it illustrates the vast contrast in mode of living alongside Olivia at the Old Boathouse in Myrtle Bay, Ventnor, back in Britain. Number 2823 is the substantial two-storey building just past the pink house. Kathleen's old home on the site was razed to the ground about 30 years ago. (image from Google Earth).

In recounting the lives of the four Parkes siblings in Vancouver, one is bound to wonder whether or not any contact was maintained with sister Olivia as the sole survivor of the family unit in Britain, for Mary Parkes, the children's paternal grandmother, had died in 1913, the same year that her son Joseph died in Vancouver. Moreover, two of Mary's daughters had pre-deceased her and the one daughter surviving had emigrated to New Zealand.

Olivia had probably left Walsall some years before she is recorded as living in Bloomsbury in 1911. In other words, their ways had been parted for a fair time. However, it seems that in those early years of separation and in the wake of the remaining siblings leaving to settle in Canada, there was some sort of contact, if only to exchange addresses or Christmas greetings. The postcard below, (courtesy Doug Brock), written in Olivia's characteristic hand (signed Cissy), reveals that she had written to Frank, but her letter was returned undelivered. The postcard itself is addressed to sister Kathleen (Dear K.) who was married to Robert Brown. It was sent to Vancouver in January 1920, and Olivia is sorry about the news that Nora has lost Edna, her first-born.

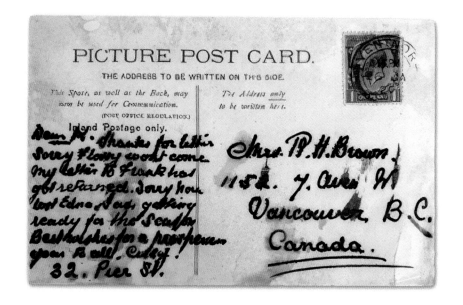

January 1920 was actually the month that Olivia moved into her shop on Pier Street in the town, for she remarks how she is just getting ready for the new season. It appears from what is said at the beginning that Olivia had tried to persuade Florence (Flossie) to come back to England and help her run the shop (bearing in mind that several of the sisters had run a sweet shop in Walsall in the early 1900s). However, it is clear that the answer was negative. In other words, the die was cast. For the rest of her life, Olivia was to remain bereft of close relatives in the country of her birth. Thousands of miles of continent and ocean now separated Olivia from her one surviving brother and her three sisters.

This is the image on the front of the card that Olivia sent to sister Kathleen on 26th January 1920. The card would probably have come from Billy Nigh's shop at 50 High Street in Ventnor, for Olivia later sent to Kathleen a WJ Nigh lettercard that included more Ventnor photos

One very much later piece of evidence of contact between the siblings is an announcement of brother Frank's death in Vancouver General Hospital in 1956 that appeared in the Isle of Wight County Press for 28th July 1956. It seems that sister Kathleen had sent it to the newspaper in the hope that Olivia would see it or be made aware of it. Another piece of evidence is found in the announcement of Frank's death in a Vancouver newspaper: it records Olivia Parkes as a surviving sibling in the Isle of Wight, England, along with Kathleen and Florence in Vancouver.

After Olivia died in January 1962, there was a general awareness in the town that she had close relatives in Canada. But how far her other two siblings were by that time really aware of Olivia's chosen mode of living is much harder to establish. On the face of it, the lives of the three sisters could hardly have been more different. One would never have imagined that they once all grew up in that same middle-class household on Wednesbury Road in Walsall at the close of the nineteenth century, more than sixty years before.

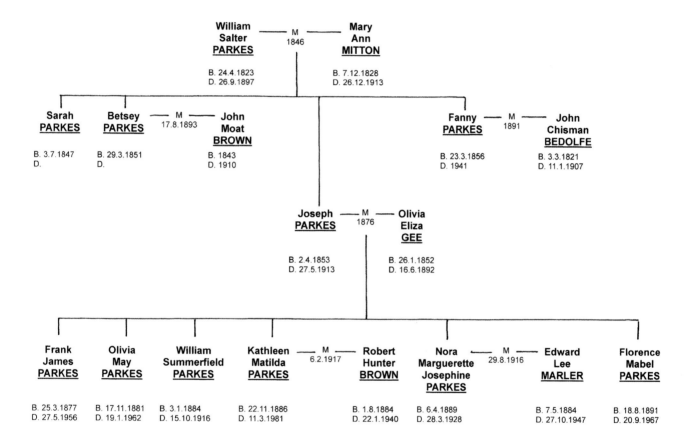

The family tree reproduced above shows Olivia May Parkes, also known in Ventnor as Britannia, down in bottom left, the second-born of the six children of Joseph Parkes and his wife, Olivia Eliza. The top portion of the tree shows Olivia's paternal grandparents and the three sisters of Joseph Parkes, Olivia's aunts.

GRANDMOTHER KATHLEEN BROWN (NEE PARKES)
MEMENTO

This was your Great Grandfather Joseph Parkes measuring device for Saddlery dimensions in 1/16", 1/8, 1/4, 1/5" of an inch. There is also an odd dimension on the outer edge of 100 division of ten units of 10. I measure it and found 10 units is exactly 3 centimeters and the full scale is 30 centimeters therefore 1 foot.

He was a highly successful Saddlery merchant and his son Frank worked with him. The Boer War demanded not only saddles but harness and ancillary horse drawn equipment, cavalry etc. Government contracts were placed for huge quantites but without supplying any funds, this was the duty of the Supplier. The war suddenly ceased the Government didn't pay for their contract orders. The result was loss of business and all else. He and Frank came to Canada. Where they laboured in Manitoba, Alberta and finally British Columbia to obtain sufficient money to provide passage for his daughters to Canada and Vancouver. Of the four, three came Kathleen, (Flossie") Florence and Norah. "Cissie" was stage struck and remained in England later passed away on the "Isle of Wight" in Ventor on 15th of January, 1962.

The image above (courtesy Doug Brock) shows Kathleen Brown's (née Parkes) family memento as dictated to one of her sons-in-law. It tells the story of Joseph's ironfounding business, its collapse after the Boer War, and then the family's emigration to Canada. But Olivia (Cissy) was the one of his children who did not leave England, for she had been 'stage-struck'. Alongside the document is Joseph Parkes's measuring device, as once used in his saddlery business.

ACKNOWLEDGEMENTS

Many individuals have assisted us in various ways in preparing this book, including Ann Barrett, Sophie Blake, Sharon Champion, Peter Cox, Kevin Digweed, Michael Gee, John Howell, Diane Landon, Sarah Miller, Ted Osborne, Les Matravers, Pauline Porteous, Lynne Siequien, Ken Trowbridge, Stefan Wells, Jill Wearing, Bernard Wood. We have also greatly benefited from the files of the late Fay Brown, now held in Ventnor Heritage Centre.

We would like to thank Les Matravers for making available the results of her researches on Olivia as part of Teresa Grimaldi and Sarah Vardy's Arts Council England project, as well as for reading and commenting on a draft of the book and helping us with further research enquiries. Les has also assisted us in getting clearance to reproduce pictures posted on the Ventnor and District Facebook Group, for which she is the administrator.

We have had the benefit of expert advice from a number of archivists, including Simon Dear at the Isle of Wight Record Office, Sharon Walz at Vancouver City Archives in British Columbia, and Libby Warren at Walsall Archives in the UK.

Finally, we must offer very special thanks to Doug Brock and Lauren Johnstone in Vancouver for making available to us a wealth of Parkes family memorabilia. Doug is a grandson of Kathleen Brown, née Parkes, while Lauren is a great grand-daughter. Their keen interest in the project sustained our efforts in the later stages of research. They have patiently ransacked closets to unearth a wonderful array of photos, documents and letters. This book would not have been the same without their input and their constant enthusiasm.

PICTURE CREDITS:

All images are credited on the pages where they appear. VHC stands for Ventnor Heritage Centre, the headquarters of the Ventnor & District Local History Society, a registered UK charity no. 286848 (www.ventnorheritage.org.uk)

LIST OF RESEARCH SOURCES:

Ancestry.co.uk, Findmypast.co.uk, Scotlandspeople.gov.uk

Commonwealth War Graves Commission

Isle of Wight Family History Society

Isle of Wight Record Office, Vancouver City Archives, Ventnor Heritage Centre, Walsall Archives

National Archives.gov.uk, H.M. Courts and Tribunal Services.gov.uk, General Register Office.gov.uk

Naval-history.net

Daily Mail, Isle of Wight County Press, Isle of Wight Observer, Isle of Wight Mercury, John Bull, Newspapers. com, Portsmouth Evening News, The Times, Vancouver Sun, Walsall Advertiser, Walsall Observer

A very grainy image of Britannia (Olivia) taken when she was well in to her seventies, not far from her hut in Myrtle Bay. In the last years of her life, around the time when she was forcibly re-housed, there was a sense in which she found herself centre-stage, especially when press and television reporters, with their cameramen and film crews, sought to profile her extraordinary abode (image courtesy of Blake's Longshoreman's Museum).